Wild Turkeys

Other titles in the Returning Wildlife series include:

The Bald Eagle
Bats
Manatees
The North American Beaver
The North American Bison
North American River Otters

Special Thanks To:

Chris Barone, USDA Forest Service

Jed Burt, Ohio Wesleyan University

Dennis C. Daniel, USDA Forest Service/National Wild Turkey Federation

Tom Hughes, National Wild Turkey Federation

James Inglis, Pheasants Forever

Dr. David A. Swanson, Ohio Department of Natural Resources Division of Wildlife

Returning Wildlife

Wild Turkeys

John E. Becker

KIDHAVEN
PRESS™

THOMSON

GALE

San Diego • Detroit • New York • San Francisco • Cleveland
New Haven, Conn. • Waterville, Maine • London • Munich

To Aunt Ruth, who shared her love of books with me.

© 2003 by KidHaven Press. KidHaven Press is an imprint of The Gale Group, Inc.,
a division of Thomson Learning, Inc.

KidHaven™ and Thomson Learning™ are trademarks used herein under license.

For more information, contact
KidHaven Press
27500 Drake Rd.
Farmington Hills, MI 48331-3535
Or you can visit our Internet site at http://www.gale.com

LIBRARY OF CONGRESS CATALOGING-IN-PUBLICATION DATA

Becker, John E., 1942–
     Wild turkeys / by John E. Becker
 p. cm. — (Returning wildlife)
 Includes bibliographical references (p.).
 Summary: Discusses the near extinction, return, and future of wild turkeys.
     ISBN 0-7377-1288-0 (hardback : alk. paper)
     1. Wild turkey—Juvenile literature. 2. Endangered species—Juvenile literature.
 3. Birds, Protection of—Juvenile literature. [1. Wild turkey. 2. Turkeys
 3. Endangered species. 4. Birds—Protection.] I. Title. II. Series.
     QUL696.G27 B43 2003
     598.6'45—dc21

 2002003810

Printed in the United States of America

Contents

chapter 1

North American Bird

Wild turkeys steadily declined in numbers from the beginning of European settlement in North America until early in the twentieth century. In the 1930s the U.S. government provided funding for programs to help wild turkeys recover. Thereafter, turkeys were live-trapped and released into areas from where they had disappeared. Soon, turkeys were reintroduced into various states and their population began to increase. Since the end of World War II, wild turkeys have made a dramatic comeback. They are now found in large numbers throughout their former range, and they are even spreading into parts of America that they had never occupied before.

Ancient Birds

Fossils reveal that wild turkeys have existed for at least 11 million years. Ancient wild turkey bones have been discovered in numerous locations across North America, but in no other part of the world.

The scientific name for the wild turkeys of the United States, *Meleagris gallopavo,* means guinea fowl–peafowl. It is a good name because turkeys are related to guinea fowl, peafowl, chickens, pheasants, and quail.

Before Europeans settled in North America, wild turkeys were found from southern Canada, throughout the eastern, central, and southwestern portions of what is now the United States, and into central Mexico.

A wild turkey flaunts its feathers as it crosses a snowy path.

Turkeys Worldwide

Native Americans **domesticated** turkeys around two thousand years ago. The Anasazi of the American Southwest, whose culture dated from A.D. 46, were one of the first tribes to raise turkeys.

Sometime after A.D. 1100, the Aztecs of Mexico first bred the domestic turkeys now found throughout the world. As early as 1511, Spanish **conquistadors** began taking turkeys they had received from the Aztecs back to Spain. Turkeys quickly spread to other countries and were established across Europe by 1530. From Europe, turkeys were introduced to many other parts of the

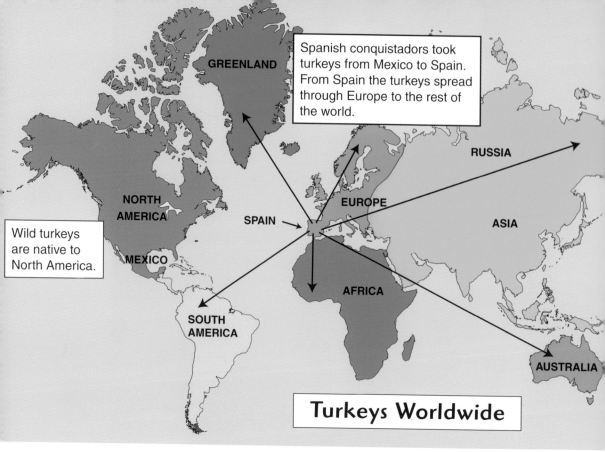

GREENLAND

Spanish conquistadors took turkeys from Mexico to Spain. From Spain the turkeys spread through Europe to the rest of the world.

RUSSIA

NORTH AMERICA

EUROPE

ASIA

SPAIN

Wild turkeys are native to North America.

MEXICO

AFRICA

SOUTH AMERICA

AUSTRALIA

Turkeys Worldwide

world, including South America, Hawaii, Russia, the Middle East, Asia, Africa, Australia, and New Zealand.

The Importance of Turkeys in Nature

Wild turkeys play an important role in nature by eating a wide variety of plants, animals, and insects. Turkeys are especially helpful in controlling insect population. Young turkeys from birth to four weeks of age, called **poults**, eat insects such as beetles, true bugs, grasshoppers, and leafhoppers.

Adult turkeys will eat almost anything they find. They prefer to eat plants such as poison ivy and grasses, as well as berries and nuts. But they will also eat animals such as tadpoles and lizards, or insects such as beetles and ants. Turkeys will even eat other birds that they come across by chance, such as finches. In winter months, turkeys consume high-energy foods such as acorns, pine seeds, and beechnuts. They will also eat grain that is left in the fields after crops have been harvested if other foods are not available.

Like other animals that eat seeds, turkeys help plants spread into new areas when the seeds pass through their digestive systems and into their droppings. By consuming cherries, for example, and distributing the seeds over a wide area, turkeys help cherry trees grow in new areas.

Turkeys also become food for a wide variety of predators such as raccoons, opossums, foxes, bobcats, rodents, snakes, coyotes, eagles, owls, and hawks.

Offspring

Wild turkeys, like other prey species, produce a large number of offspring. A female turkey, called a hen, lays an average of eleven eggs in the spring. She **incubates**

Grasshoppers, poison ivy, acorns, and beetles (clockwise from top left) are all part of a turkey's diet.

her eggs for four weeks. After the poults hatch, the hen will move her **brood** to an area with tall grass and overhanging trees as protection from predators. Most hens will defend their offspring vigorously, but for every ten poults born, only about three or four will survive to become adults.

Social Animals

Turkeys are social animals by nature. They flock together in groups as large as fifty birds, allowing them to keep careful watch for predators. They have a definite social organization with a dominant male and a dominant

A turkey chick carefully scans the area for danger.

female that control the other turkeys within the flock. After the dominant turkey, the other turkeys maintain a strict pecking order (birds of higher status peck, or dominate, the birds of lower status). Generally, only the dominant male is permitted to breed with his choice of hens.

Turkeys can adapt to many different **habitats**. Turkeys can live in forests and open prairies. They can also live in corn, wheat, and soybean fields.

Wild turkeys are well adapted to their environment. Every aspect of a wild turkey's body and senses help it avoid predators. A turkey can run up to twelve miles an hour, which allows it to outrun some predators or get a running start so it can fly away from others.

Male wild turkeys, called gobblers, stand more than forty inches tall (a little taller than a yardstick) and females stand more than thirty inches tall. Being tall allows turkeys to stretch their necks above high plants to spot predators.

Built to Survive

Turkeys come in a wide variety of colors, but are generally brown, which helps to camouflage them against a background of trees and bushes. Feathers may be any combination of brown, purple, green, bronze, red, and blue. Gobblers are especially colorful during the spring mating season, when they puff up and strut to attract the attention of females. At that time, gobblers' wattles (folds of skin underneath its chin) and caruncles (a strange-looking fleshy mass of skin on a turkey's head) glow in **iridescent** shades of red, white, and blue, giving them an impressive appearance.

Gobblers have sharp spurs on their legs that they use for fighting other gobblers or for defense if attacked by a predator. The spurs are so sharp that some Native Americans used them as arrowheads.

A wild turkey's multicolored body helps it blend into its environment.

Keen eyesight is very important to wild turkey survival. Wild turkeys can spot the slightest movement from more than one hundred yards (the length of a football field) away. Because its eyes are on the side of its head, a turkey can see in almost a complete circle with just a slight turn of its head.

Wild turkeys also have very good hearing. They can hear sounds at greater distances than people can. Their ability to accurately locate a predator from a slight sound is remarkable. Even a muffled sound by a hunter will cause a group of wild turkeys to take flight.

Wild turkeys make a wide range of sounds. Scientists have found that turkeys use sounds to communicate with each other in a way that may tell poults to freeze, or for a flock to scatter at the approach of a predator. "Peeping" sounds made by chicks before they hatch tell mother turkeys that the chicks hear them and that it is time to keep a close watch on the eggs.

Young turkeys use a whistling sound when they are lost. Roosting turkeys yelp in the morning to greet each other. The cluck is used to attract the attention of a distant turkey. The cackle is used as a signal by a hen to her chicks or to other hens to fly down from a roost. The purr is a contented sound between turkeys as if in conversation. Turkeys will make a rattling sound as they prepare to fight. The hissing sound by a hen will direct the attention of her poults to food. And the familiar

A turkey chick gets a better view of its surroundings by standing on its mother's back.

"gobble, gobble, gobble" sounds of adult gobblers help attract the attention of hens during the breeding season.

Strong, Fast Flyers

Turkeys can quickly take to the air at the first sign of danger. Turkeys are very strong flyers over short distances. They can fly at speeds up to fifty-five miles per hour for approximately one mile. Young poults, by the time they are two weeks old, can fly into the branches of a tree. Like other birds, wild turkeys fly into trees to roost for the night to stay out of reach of most predators. Despite their ability to fly, turkeys do not **migrate** during the winter. They are extremely hardy birds and are quite capable of surviving severe winter weather.

Despite their wariness, speed of flight, and community protection, wild turkeys fell victim to overhunting and habitat loss. By the twentieth century, wild turkeys had almost disappeared across America.

chapter 2

A Species in Decline

Wild turkeys are more likely to suffer large losses in numbers than other animals for a number of reasons. First, turkeys are hunted both by animals and humans for food. Second, turkeys are easy to hunt because they feed on the ground and are large birds. And finally, turkeys' habit of flocking in large groups makes them easy to spot.

Early Decline

It is estimated that between 7 million and 10 million wild turkeys lived in North America when the first Europeans arrived. Native Americans had hunted wild turkeys for centuries and the early settlers soon discovered that wild turkeys were a good source of food. The story of the Pilgrims' Thanksgiving celebration in 1621 is a well-known example of early colonists eating wild turkeys. As more and more settlers arrived from Europe and the colonies expanded inland from the Atlantic Ocean, turkeys were killed in greater numbers.

As early as 1708 a law was passed in New York Colony to protect wild turkeys in Suffolk, Queens, and Kings counties. Other colonies had no laws for the protection of turkeys. Therefore, wild turkeys were killed throughout the colonial period with little concern about their decreasing numbers.

The steady decline in wild turkey populations continued as the new Republic of the United States expanded its frontiers westward in the late 1700s. Some

15

Pilgrims pray before serving fresh wild turkey at the first Thanksgiving dinner.

Americans, however, recognized how important the wild turkey had been to the development of the young country. After the bald eagle was chosen as the symbol of the United States in 1782, Benjamin Franklin voiced the opinion that the wild turkey would have made a better choice.

Another factor in the disappearance of wild turkeys was loss of habitat. Wherever settlers went they immediately set about cutting down trees to create farmland. Those trees were a vitally important part of wild turkey habitat; without good habitat turkeys could not survive. By 1800 wild turkeys were already rare in several states.

Widespread Disappearance

In 1803 the United States bought the Louisiana Territory from France and America doubled in size. The vast new area west of the Mississippi River contained valuable minerals, huge grazing areas for cattle, rich farmland, and an abundance of wild animals. After Meriwether Lewis and William Clark explored the Louisiana Purchase land from 1804 to 1806, they told of the rich natural resources found there. Soon after, adventurers and settlers began flooding into the area. They encountered huge **flocks** of wild turkeys. It was not uncommon

Some Americans wanted the symbol of the United States to be the wild turkey instead of the bald eagle.

for settlers to report seeing flocks containing hundreds of wild turkeys, and some flocks were thought to number more than one thousand birds.

Stories of "turkey shoots," in which a hundred or more turkeys were shot in a single hunt, were common through the early part of the nineteenth century. Over time, however, constant hunting began to take its toll and fewer large flocks of wild turkeys were seen.

Sacajawea leads Lewis and Clark on an expedition through the Rocky Mountains.

At that same time, the hunting of wild turkeys continued in the eastern sections of the country. Wild turkeys were becoming rare, but most Americans still believed that turkeys were an endless resource that could be taken whenever and wherever they were found. Some states, however, were beginning to feel the effects of allowing people to hunt wild turkeys without restrictions. Connecticut reported that the last wild turkey disappeared from that state in 1813. New York lost its last wild turkey in 1844. And Massachusetts had no wild turkeys after 1851. Consequently, by the mid-1800s turkeys had been completely eliminated in many sections of the eastern part of the country. Where wild turkeys managed to survive, they were greatly reduced in numbers.

Recognizing that wild turkeys were beginning to disappear in the West as they had in the East, lawmakers began to take action in an attempt to protect wild turkeys. Missouri passed a law in 1851 protecting wild turkeys in St. Louis County. And Nebraska passed a law in 1860 to protect wild turkeys in that state.

Market Hunting

The turkeys that managed to survive being hunted by individual hunters during the middle of the nineteenth century soon fell victim to a much greater threat. Groups of professional hunters, hired by businesspeople to kill all the turkeys they could find, began shooting wild turkeys relentlessly. This practice, known as market hunting, almost drove the species to extinction. Market hunting was introduced to supply meat for the rapidly growing cities across America.

Market hunting reached its peak after the Civil War, when many former soldiers turned to hunting to earn an income. By the last two decades of the nineteenth century, American wild turkeys were also being shipped to other countries. In 1881 a St. Louis exporting company sent seven hundred turkeys to London to satisfy the demand for turkey meat in England.

The slaughter of wild turkeys continued into the early part of the twentieth century. Some people were beginning to see the effect that market hunting was having on wildlife. Sport hunters opposed hunting to supply markets, arguing that it would eventually cause wild turkeys to disappear completely.

Early Rescue Attempts Fail

By 1907 Kansas, South Dakota, Ohio, Nebraska, Wisconsin, Michigan, Illinois, Indiana, and Iowa had also lost their wild turkeys. At that time, many people joined sport hunters in raising the alarm about the disappearance of wild turkeys. The growing concern prompted states to seek ways to protect turkeys and increase their numbers. Very little information was known about turkeys, however. Consequently, people thought that farm-raised turkeys could simply be released in the same areas as wild turkeys.

A number of states began to collect eggs from the nests of wild turkeys and take the eggs to game farms. The game farms had success in hatching young turkeys from the eggs and were able to raise large numbers of captive turkeys. The game-farm turkeys were then released into the wild with the hope that they would live in the areas where wild turkeys had disappeared.

It soon became clear that game-farm turkeys, raised in fenced areas by humans, lacked many of the important survival skills that mother hens teach their offspring in the wild. Game-farm turkeys had no experience finding food on their own, had no one to teach them how to avoid predators, or even how to fly into a tree to roost

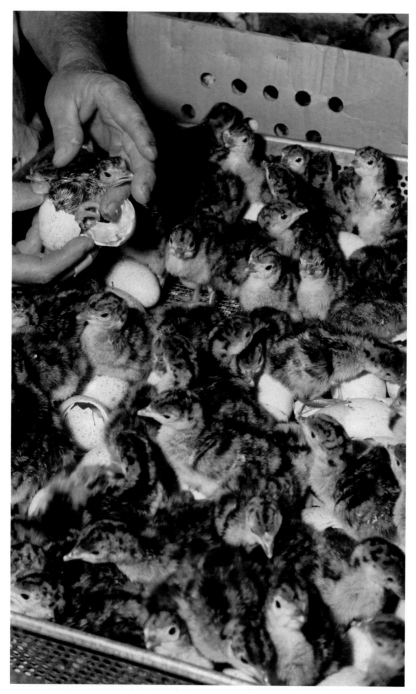

As game-farm turkey chicks pop out of their warm eggs, a farmer takes them to be raised in fenced enclosures.

Game-farm turkeys gather at feeding time.

safely at night. They also had no guidance from their
mothers to help them build a nest, or how to raise offspring of their own. Therefore, in almost every case,
game-farm turkeys died after being released into the
wild. And the millions of dollars spent by states to
restore wild turkeys were lost.

An even greater problem with releasing game-farm
turkeys into the wild was that some of the released
birds mingled with wild turkeys. Those that bred with
wild turkeys produced offspring that were not strong
enough to survive in the wild. And in some instances,
game-farm turkeys carried diseases that caused healthy
wild turkeys to become sick and die.

By any measure, the use of game-farm turkeys to restore wild turkey populations was a disaster that set back wild turkey recovery efforts by at least twenty years. Therefore, as people continued hunting wild turkeys, their populations continued to decline throughout the first half of the twentieth century. By 1949 wild turkeys had disappeared from nineteen states, and were in trouble in the states where they could still be found.

Could Wild Turkeys Be Saved?

When the numbers of wild turkeys declined, hunters stopped hunting them. The remaining turkeys, holding on in remote areas throughout their former range, had a chance of surviving. But was it too late? Sport hunters and other **conservationists** did not believe so. They combined to put pressure on the federal government to take an active role in the restoration of wild turkeys.

chapter 3

The Long Road Back

Returning wild turkeys to areas from where they had disappeared was not an easy task. It took the combined efforts of state and federal agencies, as well as a number of private conservation organizations, many years before wild turkeys began to recover.

States Take the Lead

Early efforts to stop the decline in wild turkey populations rested with the states. States began passing laws in the late 1800s to restrict hunting by establishing hunting seasons (allowing the hunting of turkeys only during certain times of the year) and **bag limits** (allowing a certain number of turkeys to be taken at one time). In 1875 Arkansas became the first state to pass a law outlawing market hunting. In 1878, Iowa was the first state to pass a bag limit law. By 1880 every state had passed some type of law protecting **game birds**. Unfortunately, those laws were not well enforced and turkey populations continued to decline. Those efforts did, however, represent the beginning of wildlife conservation practices that would eventually help save wild turkeys.

Conservation Through Wise Use

Early in the twentieth century President Theodore Roosevelt developed a new philosophy about people's relationship with the natural world. That philosophy was "conservation through wise use." President Roosevelt believed that natural resources, such as water, forests,

President Theodore Roosevelt involved the federal government in efforts to conserve natural resources.

rangelands, and wildlife, could last forever if people would use those resources wisely. The key was to allow the resources to renew themselves at a rate faster than they were being harvested.

In the 1930s, the conservation movement, inspired by President Roosevelt and enthusiastically supported by sportsmen and others, succeeded in persuading the federal government to take action to help turkeys. Two

25

historic pieces of legislation passed in that decade changed the way in which wildlife would be managed in the United States forever. In 1935 the Cooperative Wildlife Research Unit Program created a system whereby wildlife professionals were trained to manage and protect wildlife across the country.

Two years later, the Federal Aid in Wildlife Restoration Act was approved. That act is commonly referred to as the Pittman-Robertson Act for the two congressmen who sponsored it—Senator Key Pittman of Nevada and Representative A. Willis Robertson of Virginia. The act provided the money for states to hire these newly trained wildlife professionals and get them into the field.

The stage was set for wild turkeys to recover, but it would be several more years before wild turkey populations increased.

Wild Turkeys Return

In 1935 fifteen wild turkeys were live-trapped in New Mexico and released in Wyoming. (By 1958, those birds increased to ten thousand.) A few years later, twenty-nine wild turkeys were captured in New Mexico and Colorado and released in South Dakota. (By 1960, those birds had increased to between five thousand and seven thousand.) Other western states began similar trap-release projects during the 1930s and 1940s with encouraging results.

Projects to live-trap and release wild turkeys in the eastern part of the country were not as successful. Turkeys of the Southwest seemed to be much more willing to walk into open-fronted, or walk-in, traps, than the more cautious turkeys of the East. But in 1948 small cannons were used to shoot nets over flocks of turkeys.

A wild turkey (right) scouts its new environment after being relocated.

Scientists have done studies on wild turkeys' needs to help make sure they grow to be big and strong.

This method worked well, making it possible to relocate eastern wild turkeys in large numbers.

Although improved trapping techniques played a key role in helping wild turkeys, other factors were just as important. Before turkeys could be restored, habitat needed to improve. Both federal and state forestry agencies worked to increase habitat for turkeys. Scientific studies of the feeding habits and habitat needs of wild turkeys were started. Understanding turkeys and their basic survival needs helped make restoration efforts successful in many states.

The state of Mississippi, for example, historically had large numbers of wild turkeys. But unrestricted logging and hunting during the early part of the twentieth century caused turkeys to disappear from Mississippi.

As early as 1918, concerned sportsmen in Mississippi attempted to breed domestic hens with wild gobblers to increase numbers. But the effort did not work because the offspring were half domestic and not strong enough to survive in the wild.

By 1932 wild turkeys were almost extinct in Mississippi. That year, the Mississippi Game and Fish Commission was founded, and it tried different methods to restore the wild turkey population. In 1940 wild turkeys were trapped in parts of the state and relocated to other areas with habitat the turkeys preferred. In just two years, Mississippi's wild turkey population rose to five thousand. By 1987 wild turkeys were common in almost every area of Mississippi, and nearly a half million birds were living in the state.

Ohio's experience was repeated in other states in the Midwest. Turkeys had completely disappeared from Ohio by 1904. The first attempt to restore wild turkeys to that state between 1952 and 1957 failed because game-farm turkeys were used for the project. Thereafter, wild turkeys from other states were successfully released in Ohio. Today, the wild turkey population in Ohio has grown to more than a quarter million.

Wild turkeys have not only come back in states from which they had disappeared, but have also been introduced into states where they had not existed previously. Wild turkeys are now found in every state in the United States except Alaska.

Organizations Helping Wild Turkeys

Within the federal government a number of agencies have played an important role in helping wild turkeys recover. Some of the most important agencies have been the U.S. Department of Agriculture, Forest Service, U.S. Department of Interior, Bureau of Land Management, and U.S.

A wildlife officer holds a wild turkey while another tags it.

Fish and Wildlife Service. These agencies manage large areas of wild turkey habitat across the United States. By managing that land with the protection of wild turkeys in mind, these agencies are protecting turkey habitat so that wild turkeys can continue to breed and prosper.

The U.S. Army has also played a role in wild turkey restoration. In 1983 and 1985 the army assisted in the transfer of wild turkeys from Mexico to the American Southwest.

International cooperation has helped increase the numbers of wild turkeys in Canada. Turkeys imported into Ontario from Missouri, Iowa, Michigan, New York, Vermont, and New Jersey helped Canada's wild turkey population to more than triple in five years. Wild turkeys are now also found in Quebec, Manitoba, Saskatchewan, and British Columbia.

Private organizations, such as National Wild Turkey Federation (NWTF), are also making significant contributions to wild turkey conservation. Since NWTF was founded in 1973, it has raised more than $144 million

An excited crowd cheers as a turkey is released into the wild.

for projects that benefit wild turkeys. That money provides funding for improvements to wild turkey habitat, projects to return wild turkeys to areas from where they had disappeared, classes to teach children and adults how to hunt safely, law enforcement, research projects, and land purchase. In 2001 NWTF contributed more than $1 million for land purchase, most of which will be managed by state wildlife agencies. Since 1987 NWTF has helped to acquire more than 153,000 acres of land, which is being managed for wild turkey habitat.

An Amazing Recovery

The recovery of wild turkeys across the United States has been amazingly successful. Many states are now approaching, or have already surpassed, the population levels that existed before European settlement. More remarkable is the fact that wild turkeys have been established in many parts of the country where they did not exist before. Given the tremendous success of this restoration project, there is widespread optimism about the future of wild turkeys in America.

chapter 4

Heading in the Right Direction

Two wildlife officers from the Missouri Department of Conservation remained perfectly still while peering through the small opening of the well-camouflaged **blind**. Outside, a flock of wild turkeys followed a trail of corn that ended near the blind. The turkeys hungrily ate the corn and did not notice the barrels of three small cannons aimed over their heads. As the turkeys crowded together to gobble up the last remnants of the corn, one of the wildlife officers slowly pressed the button to fire the cannons.

A wildlife conservation officer peeks out from behind a bush as he waits to trap a turkey for relocation.

"Blam, blam, blam." Three loud explosions, followed by the frantic shrieks of the turkeys, filled the air. Before the turkeys could escape, they were captured beneath a huge net that had been catapulted over them by the cannons.

Immediately, the two wildlife officers raced from the blind and began collecting the dazed birds. In a matter of minutes, all of the birds were caught and safely deposited in crates that were waiting to transport them to their new home.

A group of turkeys explore their new home after being released into the wild.

Many similar captures have been carried out across the country as turkeys have been relocated from one area to another. Because of trap-release projects such as these, wild turkeys are now firmly reestablished across North America.

Concerns Remain

The restoration of wild turkeys has been so successful that it is hard to imagine that the species could ever be in trouble again. Scientists who have monitored the rise of wild turkey populations, however, point out that the loss of suitable habitat could, once again, result in the disappearance of turkeys. As human populations continue to grow, wildlife habitat continues to disappear. Wild turkeys can adapt to a variety of habitats, but they cannot survive in the midst of suburban development.

Another concern is **poaching**. Laws protecting wild turkeys have never been stronger, or better enforced. Unfortunately, some people disregard the law and hunt turkeys out of season, or kill more turkeys than the law allows. These poachers are not usually a significant threat to wild turkeys. But if habitat is lost and turkey populations begin to decline again, poachers could become a serious problem for the species.

Yet another threat to wild turkeys is the introduction of "new" predators into areas where they were not formerly found. An example of this problem is the spread of coyotes into the eastern sections of the country. For centuries, wolves roamed the eastern regions of what is now the United States. The presence of wolves prevented coyotes from moving eastward. Because wolves have disappeared from most of their eastern range, coyotes have gradually migrated eastward and are now common throughout the eastern states. Wolves eat turkeys only occasionally. Wolves also help turkeys by eating raccoons, which commonly raid turkey nests.

35

A coyote drags off its kill—a wild turkey.

Coyotes, on the other hand, will seek out turkeys to eat and normally do not attack raccoons. As coyote populations steadily increase in the East, scientists are carefully watching to see what effect they will have on wild turkey populations.

Ongoing Projects

One way that people are working to ensure that wild turkeys thrive is by buying land for turkeys. The most effective way to protect wild turkey habitat is to place it in the hands of governmental agencies. The purchase

36

of prime wild turkey habitat by states, or lease agreements between private landowners and state agencies, helps ensure that the land will remain good turkey habitat.

Some conservationists are changing land areas so that turkeys can live on them. Some old fields, for example, may be too overgrown with weeds and other tall grasses that turkeys cannot eat. Those fields may be mowed or burned to allow new plants to grow. Areas with drainage ditches and dikes may need to be altered to allow flooding so that the land does not become unnaturally dry.

The way that trees are cut down can either create good wild turkey habitat or make an area unfit for

A wild turkey walks through tall grass that will eventually be cleared by conservationists.

turkeys. Clear-cutting, cutting down all of the trees in a section of the forest, can leave good turkey habitat if the cuts are not too large. If all the trees are removed from a large section of forest, turkeys do not have places to hide from predators or enough food to eat. Turkeys do best in areas where there is a balance of young and old trees.

Historically, wild turkeys were distributed throughout the eastern and central portions of the United States. Today, wild turkeys are being introduced into

A clear-cut forest can mean too little food and no hiding places for wild turkeys.

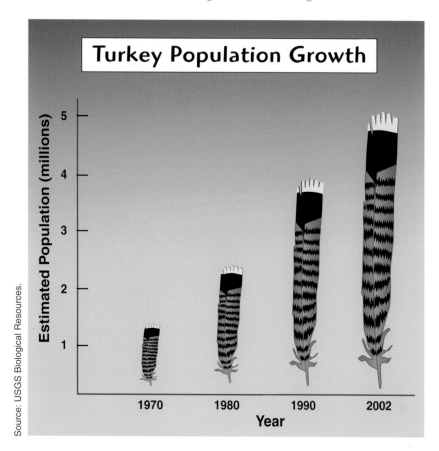

Turkey Population Growth

Source: USGS Biological Resources.

many new areas and are well established in all the western states. Even Hawaii has a growing population of wild turkeys.

Help for Wild Turkeys

Moving wild turkeys from areas where they are plentiful into areas from where they have disappeared will continue into the future. Finding less stressful ways to capture turkeys, therefore, is an important goal. One technique for capturing wild turkeys that is increasing in popularity is using drugs that cause turkeys to become sleepy and be easily caught. There are several advantages to using this technique including lower cost, no need to use bait, and fewer people are needed.

Scientific studies continue to provide valuable information that helps biologists restore wild turkeys. Much more can be learned, however, especially through studies of wild turkeys that are conducted over long periods of time. Long-term studies give scientists increased understanding of how turkeys fare in certain habitat conditions, how changes in climate affect turkeys, what foods increase turkeys' chances of survival, and the role various predators play in the decline of wild turkey populations. From these studies, biologists can apply sound management strategies to ensure that wild turkeys continue to flourish.

Children across the country are also actively involved in the conservation of wild turkeys. NWTF's

People gather to watch as a wild turkey is set free at a Thanksgiving Day turkey release.

JAKES (Juniors Acquiring Knowledge, Ethics, and Sportsmanship) program is specifically aimed at youngsters seventeen years old and younger. Through the JAKES program, children learn the importance of wildlife conservation and the wise use of all of our natural resources.

In some places, children are actually helping to restore wild turkeys. In Ohio, for example, children have been given the privilege of releasing wild turkeys that have been captured in one area and relocated to another.

Wild Turkeys Firmly Reestablished

Wild turkeys are now firmly reestablished in most of their former range in the United States. They are also spreading into parts of the country where they were not known to exist prior to European settlement. More than 5.6 million wild turkeys roam freely in forty-nine states, giving the species a bright outlook for the future.

bag limit: Limits set on the number of animals a hunter may capture at one time.

blind: A structure built by hunters or conservationists to conceal themselves.

brood: The offspring of a female bird.

conquistadors: The Spanish conquerors of the Americas.

conservationist: A person who supports the conservation of natural resources.

domesticated: Tamed to live with or be used by humans.

flock: A group of birds.

fossil: Preserved remains of a living creature from another geological age.

game bird: Any bird hunted for sport.

habitat: The locality or living space of a plant or animal.

incubate: To sit on eggs so that they will hatch.

iridescent: Exhibiting rainbowlike colors.

migrate: To move from one area to another, especially seasonally.

poaching: Taking game or endangered animals illegally.

poult: The stage of growth for a turkey from birth to four weeks of age.

Books and Periodicals

Jim Arnosky, *All About Turkeys*. New York: Scholastic Press, 1998. Beautifully illustrated book about basic physical characteristics and behaviors of wild turkeys.

Leslie Dendy, "What Turkeys Eat for Thanksgiving," *Spider,* November 1999. Explains what both wild and domestic turkeys eat, and how they are able to digest foods such as nuts.

Mary Taylor Gray, "Giving Thanks for Wild Turkeys," *Falcon,* November/December 1995. Covers wild turkeys' physical characteristics and behaviors.

Sigmund A. Lavine and Vincent Scuro, *Wonders of Turkeys.* New York: Dodd, Mead, 1984. Classic book about wild and domestic turkeys, their history, behaviors, and place in folklore.

Dorothy Hinshaw Patent, *Wild Turkeys*. Minneapolis: Lerner Publications, 1999. Presents the story of wild turkeys, including their physical characteristics and behaviors, as well as information about their habitat.

Ranger Rick, "Wild Turkeys," November 2001. Interesting facts about wild turkeys, along with web addresses for further information.

David Stemple, *High Ridge Gobbler: A Story of the American Wild Turkey.* Honesdale, PA: Boyds Mills Press, 2001. Follows the life cycle of a flock of wild turkeys from birth to adulthood.

Organizations

National Wild Turkey Federation (NWTF)
PO Box 530
Edgefield, SC 29824

www.nwtf.org

This organization plays a major role in the preservation of wild turkeys through fundraising, education, and specific conservation programs aimed at the restoration of wild turkeys and their habitat.

Websites

eNature.com (www.enature.com). This site provides basic information about wild turkeys and their geographic range, and it also has an audio link to listen to wild turkey sounds.

United States Geological Survey (www.mbr-pwrc. usgs.gov). This site provides basic information about the physical characteristics and behaviors of wild turkeys.

Video

In Celebration of America's Wildlife. U.S. Fish and Wildlife Service: Publications Unit, 1987. A look at a number of wildlife species, including wild turkeys, that have been restored through the actions of concerned people across the country.

Dr. John E. Becker writes books and magazine articles about nature and wild animals for children. He graduated from Ohio State University in the field of education. He has been an elementary school teacher, college professor, zoo administrator, and has worked in the field of wildlife conservation with the International Society for Endangered Cats. He currently lives in Delaware, Ohio, and teaches writing at the Thurber Writing Academy. He also enjoys visiting schools and sharing his love of writing with kids. In his spare time, Dr. Becker likes to read, hike in the woods, ice skate, and play tennis.